CRIME SCENE SCIENCE

CRIMINAL PROFILING

By Barbara J. Davis

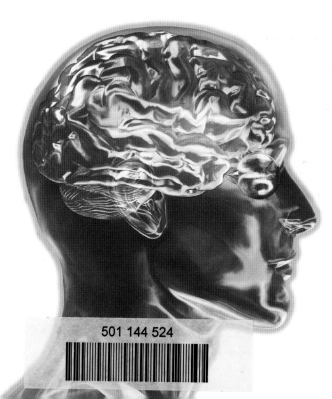

First published in Great Britain in 2007 by ticktock Media Ltd,
2 Orchard Business Centre, North Farm Road, Tunbridge Wells, Kent, TN2 3XF

ISBN-13: 978-1-84696-322-3 pbk

Printed in China

A CIP catalogue record for this book is available from the British Library.

Editor: Ruth Owen
Designer: Vicky Crichton
Picture Researcher: Lizzie Knowles

ACKNOWLEDGMENTS
The publisher extends a big thank you to Wayne Petherick, consultant criminologist,
and Brent Turvey, forensic scientist and criminal profiler, for their input and help; and
science consultant Suzy Gazlay.

PICTURE CREDITS

t = top, b = bottom, c = centre, l = left, r = right, OFC = outside front cover, OBC = outside back cover

Alamy: 9, 12c, 17br. BrandXpictures: 14, 24, 30, 38r. Corbis: 11tl, 21l. Empics: 8t, 13, 21r, 28. Rex Features: 6b, 7. Shutterstock:
OFC Background, OFC all, 1, 3, 4t, 5, 6t, 8b, 10r, 11r, 12l, 12r, 16, 18, 20, 22t, 23, 26, 27, 29, 31, 33, 34b, 35, 37, 38l, 39, 41r, 42, 43,
44, 46, 47, OBC Background, OBCt, OBCr. Science Photo Library: 10l, 17l, 19, 25, 32, 34t, 36t. Superstock: 4b, 22b, 36b, 40, 41l, OBCl.
ticktock Media Picture Archive: 15, 45.

Every effort has been made to trace the copyright holders, and we apologise in advance for any unintentional omissions.
We would be pleased to insert the appropriate acknowledgements in any subsequent edition of this publication.

CONTENTS

POLICE LINE DO NOT CROSS

To some people it seems like magic. A murder has taken place and the police don't have any idea who the murderer could be. Within a few hours a famous criminal profiler has come up with a complete personality description of the killer. In fact, the profiler just about has the criminal's name figured out. Detectives then swoop in, arrest the criminal, and bring him to justice. Case solved!

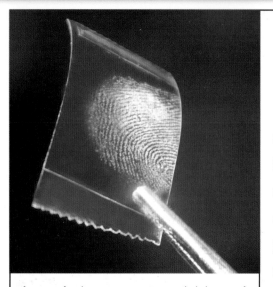

A fingerprint found at a crime scene. You may think this piece of evidence would only be of use to a detective or forensic scientist, but criminal profilers also rely on physical evidence found at crime scenes to help them in their work.

While this may make for a great TV or film storyline, the reality of criminal profiling is quite different. Profiling is not magic, and it is not a quick fix. It should be based on scientific procedures, psychology, and a thorough investigation of the crime. While the police work with suspects, statements and witnesses, a profiler approaches a crime from a different perspective. A profiler looks at the way a crime is committed and the behaviour of the perpetrator at the crime scene; both of these will reveal to the profiler things about the perpetrator's personality.

What is a profile?

A real criminal profile is a description of the characteristics and motives of a person who committed a particular crime at a particular time. A profile does not identify a specific person – although it can lead to one! Criminal profilers want to

A woman lies dead in the dramatic opening scenes of a TV crime show! In the case of a real life murder, a criminal profiler will use photographs of the victim at the crime scene to help them answer two important questions about the crime: how was the woman killed? And why was she killed?

understand how and why a crime happened. This is because profilers believe that understanding how and why will help detectives find who committed the crime.

How is profiling used?

Profiling can help focus the search for an offender and prevent the loss of precious time by steering an investigation in a particular direction. Let's say a serial killer has murdered five people over a period of two years. In that time detectives will have received thousands of 'tips' from members of the public. They may have collected thousands of pieces of evidence from the crime scenes. They may also have hundreds of possible suspects. It would take a

great deal of valuable time to follow up on each of these possible leads. This is time that the serial killer could use to murder yet another person.

A criminal profiler, however, will look at all that data in such a way as to better identify which pieces of information are most likely to lead the detectives to the perpetrator. This saves time – and saving time might just save lives!

Criminal profiling is a skill that involves the meticulous examination of a criminal's behaviour at the crime scene in order to understand what a criminal did; how the criminal did it; why the criminal did it; and how he or she may do it again in the future.

It's a popular myth that profilers can get inside the minds of criminals, but unfortunately it is just that – a myth. However, as this book will show, the real world of criminal profiling is even more fascinating than the fantasy!

PURPOSE OF A CRIMINAL PROFILE

- Help identify the perpetrator of a crime by analysing the type of crime and the way in which it was committed.

- Provide advice to the police about the way an offender might escalate into more serious crimes.

- Advise the prosecution on a strategy for the trial once an offender is caught.

H ave you ever read a biography about a famous person? A biography includes important things that happened to the person throughout his or her life and it uses facts to tell a story about an individual. A criminal profile is something like a biography in that it also presents certain facts. Unlike a biography, however, a criminal profile presents these facts about a type of person rather than one specific person.

A profile can describe to us a 'type' of person, but to give that person a face and a name – now that's much harder!

The first written criminal profile

In 1888, within a period of less than four months, five women were murdered in a poor, run-down area of London. The murders were especially violent and bloody. Each woman had been mutilated in some way. One victim's throat had been cut so deeply that her head was almost severed. Every time the killer struck, the mutilations became worse. The sheer violence of the crimes stunned the police. They had never seen anything like this before. They had no idea where to even begin to look for the perpetrator. Help came from an unlikely source – a physician named Dr. Thomas Bond.

Dr. Bond was a police surgeon. He had carried out the autopsy on the last, and most horribly mutilated, victim. Even though the mutilations were terrible, they also

A gruesome display at the London Dungeon Museum depicts the horror of the Victorian serial killer's crimes.

seemed to be done with some precision: did the killer perhaps have some surgical experience?

Bond examined all of the victims, paying close attention to certain details. He also paid close attention to the reports about the crime scenes and the photographs that had been taken. Bond then tried to reconstruct each crime. He tried to look at the crime scene evidence and the victims themselves from a different point of view: he knew the physical causes for the women's deaths – now he looked for things that might indicate why they were killed in such a vicious manner. Why would the killer cut up their bodies and take pieces away?

Bond noticed things such as evidence that the killer may have worn some type of covering on his clothing to keep his clothes clean during the bloody business of murder. This would seem to show that the murderer was a person who took some care in his personal appearance. At the very least, it showed that the killer was aware that the bloodstains would cause other people to notice his crimes. This means that the killer was not so driven by something inside his head that he totally lost contact with reality.

As the doctor examined the wounds on each of the victims, he paid attention to the exact way the cuts were made?

Did the killer use a special weapon that only someone like a doctor or butcher would use? Being a surgeon himself, Bond knew that a trained doctor would make incisions (cuts) in a particular way. Based on his observations, Bond concluded that the killer was not a person who knew anything about surgical techniques.

The front page of *The Illustrated Police News* from 6 October, 1888. The headline reads "Two more Whitechapel horrors. When will the murderer be captured?"

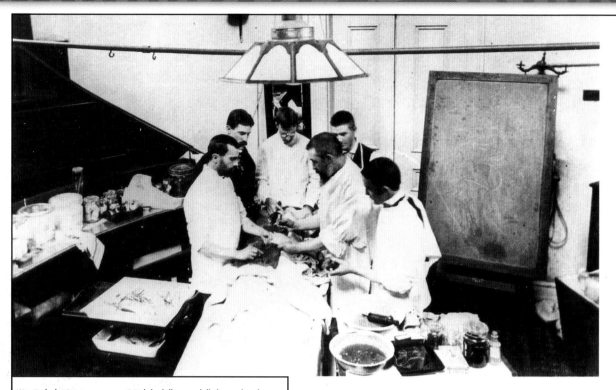

Was Jack the Ripper a surgeon? Did the killer use skills learned in the Victorian operating theatre to help him carry out his crimes? Bond said, "No." However, Dr. George Philips, another police surgeon involved with the case, disagreed. Philips felt the wounds were made by someone with surgical skill. Even today, experts can disagree when profiling a criminal!

Dr. Bond didn't know it, but he had created the first criminal profile. He had looked at the similarities in how the crimes were committed and had recognised patterns. For example, the killer always used a long knife and always took away some of the victim's internal organs, such as the liver. Looking at how the crimes were

The sheer violence of the Ripper's crimes still shock us today! Why did he cut open the stomach of one of his victims and slice out her intestines? As a surgeon Bond understood the 'how', but he was not able to fathom the 'why'.

PROFILING JACK THE RIPPER

Dr. Thomas Bond looked at many pieces of information in trying to find out more about the killer.

- Bond noticed that four of the five murders were carried out quickly and in quite open places. The fact the murders were quick would point to a physically strong man who could overpower his victims without much of a fight.

- Four of the five women had been found in alleyways close to homes and in places where other people were walking around. This seemed to show Bond that the killer was able to stay fairly calm and not get too nervous while carrying out his crimes – even though the chances of being caught in the act were quite high.

- All of the victims had been prostitutes. Bond felt this showed that the killer hated women, or hated prostitutes.

- Bond believed the killer was probably a middle-aged man who looked fairly ordinary. What led Bond to this conclusion? He based his theory partially on the knowledge that an individual who did not look fairly ordinary would have been noticed by someone who lived in the area.

A dark, London alleyway – forever associated with the Whitechapel murders of 1888. To a criminal profiler the location of the crime is extremely important. You will read more about this in Chapter 3.

carried out gave Bond some understanding about what kind of person had murdered the women.

Not all of the experts involved in the case agreed with Dr. Bond, though. For example, Dr. George Philips, the divisional police surgeon (the equivalent to a forensic pathologist today) felt that the wounds to some of the victims did show evidence of surgical knowledge. Dr. Philips thought that the wounds to Annie Chapman (the second victim) were very clean, precise and deliberate. Specifically, the murderer had been able to remove some organs without disturbing or harming others. This all suggested to Dr. Philips that the killer must have had some surgical skill.

The experts working on the case disagreed about details within the profile! This can still happen today – even to the point of two experts with opposing assessments of a criminal's characteristics taking the stand in court as expert witnesses on opposite sides of a case.

Unfortunately, Dr. Bond's profile did not lead to the capture of the killer. There was also no way to prove if Dr. Bond's profile was accurate because the killer, who became known to history as Jack the Ripper, was never captured. His killing spree ended as suddenly as it started.

People have been wondering about Jack the Ripper's identity ever since.

Lombroso's theory stated that the characteristics of 'The Born Criminal' included head size, having a large jaw and cheekbones, eye defects, large ears, large lips, unusual teeth, wrinkles, and defects to the body. Five or more of these characteristics were needed to be classified as a 'Born Criminal' type.

The word psychology comes from two Greek words – 'psyche' meaning the mind, and 'logos' meaning the study of a subject. So psychology was to become 'the study of the mind'.

The Criminologists

Over time, there have been a number of attempts to study crime and criminals to figure out what they do and why they do it. Early criminologists focused on body type and shape; others looked at genetic influences, such as why crime seemed to run in some families.

In 1876, the Italian physician Lombroso published his book *The Criminal Man*. Most experts agree that Lombroso's attempt to classify people who had committed crimes according to their physical characteristics was one of the first examples of someone trying to find a way to compare criminals. Lombroso thought that if you compared information, such as race, age, sex, education and geographic location, about criminals who had carried out similar crimes, you could better understand the

Modern day criminal profiling didn't just magically appear. It is the result of a great deal of time and work by other disciplines including criminology, psychology and forensic science.

Cesare Lombroso (1835—1909) not only carried out scientific studies of criminals, he also tried to reform the penal system in Italy by championing the humane treatment of convicts and encouraging the use of work programmes to make criminals more constructive and productive members of society.

MANY CRIMES, MANY PROFILES

The special point of view that a profiler provides is helpful in many different situations:

- Murder
- Rape
- Sexual assault
- Kidnapping
- Terrorism
- Bombing
- Hostage-taking

- Espionage (spying)
- Stalking
- Arson
- Extortion
- Burglary
- Threatening letters
- Product tampering

In the case of a crime involving one offender and multiple victims, a skilled profiler can find the thread that pulls together what looks like a series of unrelated crimes.

origins of crime and the reasons criminals do what they do.

Lombroso's criminals

Lombroso's research suggested there were three types of criminal.

The first type was 'The Born Criminal'. This type of criminal was a throw-back to earlier stages of human evolution and was very primitive in his physical characteristics. Lombroso believed that there were certain characteristics that could be used to identify a 'Born Criminal', these included head size, having long arms, and having extra fingers and toes.

The second type of criminal was 'The Insane Criminal'. Lombroso believed that these people were generally mentally ill, or suffered from some other physical or mental defect.

The third type was 'The Criminaloid', a general class of criminals who didn't have any identifiable characteristics. Although there were no recognisable defects in these criminals, it was thought that their overall makeup (both mental and physical) left them open to commit criminal acts given the right conditions.

11

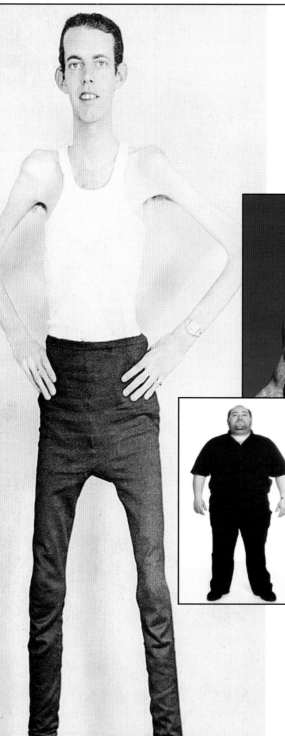

Nearly 100 years later, in the 1950s, there was another attempt made to study body types by a German psychiatrist, Ernst Kretschmer.

Kretschmer found four body types that he thought were linked with particular types of crimes. Kretschmer thought a tall, thin person was likely to be involved in minor crimes and fraud; an athletic person with well built muscles was likely to be involved in violent crime; a short, fat person might be more likely to commit crimes involving deception and fraud – they might also commit violent crimes. Kretschmer's fourth body type was anything not covered by the other three!

Of course, we now know that physical body types have nothing to do with whether a person is more or less likely to become a criminal. However, the attempts of Lombroso and Kretschmer to classify people because they had certain physical characteristics is very similar to what modern profilers do when they classify criminals because they show characteristics of being a 'type'.

The Psychologists

Psychology is the study of the mind. The first psychologists in history weren't actually psychologists though – they were philosophers.

Early philosophers questioned the workings of the human mind: when we touch a brick wall, how does our mind register what it is? How does a thought such as 'stand up' translate into a physical action 'the act of standing up'?

Tall, short, fat, thin, athletic, or none of the above! Early attempts at profiling criminals focused on physical characteristics rather than behaviour and personality.

These early thinkers believed that certain brain structures were responsible for making us act, but they did not have a good understanding of the structure of the physical human body, so another area of science became important in making the mind-body connection.

Physiology is the area of biology that is concerned with the functions and activities of living organisms. Early physiologists had a much better understanding of the structure of the human body than philosophers and were better able to conduct scientific studies to see which parts of the brain did what.

By the late 1800s, a number of philosophers and physiologists were asking questions about the human mind, but these were still related almost entirely to their own fields of study.

A new way of thinking

It wasn't until 1879 that a German professor named Wilhelm Wundt argued that there should be an entirely new discipline called psychology. This new science had its origins in both philosophy and physiology, but it was a separate scientific discipline in its own right. Over the next few decades, a number of new and independent thinkers joined this new science of psychology, and the debates really began: was the way a person thought more important than their behaviour? How do we develop thought? And what has a greater effect over our behaviour – nature or nurture? Are we born to act in certain ways (nature) or do we learn to act in certain ways (nurture)?

Eventually psychologists began to study certain groups of people like those suffering from mental disorders or personality problems. They noticed that there were certain behaviour patterns linked to certain psychological problems, and that these behaviour patterns could almost be used to predict how a person with a certain problem would act in the future.

Early philosophers and physiologists were interested to know which parts of the human brain performed which tasks. Today we know much more, but there is still much to understand. In this photograph, Dr. Helen Morrison, an expert on serial killers, examines slices of the brain of American serial killer John Wayne Gacy. The killer agreed to let Morrison, a forensic psychologist, examine his brain after his execution.

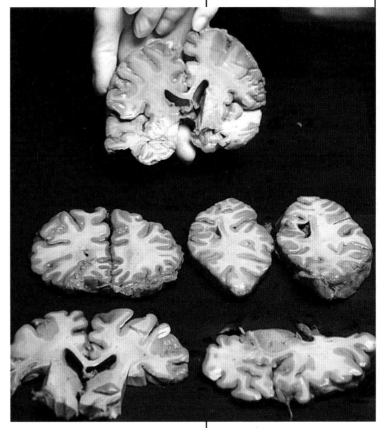

13

A police officer 'bags' a coin found at a crime scene. This simple item has just become a piece of 'physical evidence' it will now play its part in answering the question, "What happened here?"

It wasn't just mental disorders the psychologists studied, it was also the way someone's personality makes them behave. This was later to become important for criminal profiling because the way a person acts with people in their everyday life is also how they generally act with people they come into contact with when committing crimes. This area of study was to become the basis for most profiling methods.

Although there have been a number of important contributions to profiling from other areas, some of the earliest examples we have of actual profiles were done by psychiatrists, who are medical doctors with specialist training in psychology. Two of these profiles are discussed in this chapter in the case studies of Adolf Hitler (page 15) and The Mad Bomber of New York (page 20–21).

The Forensic Scientists

Forensic science is an applied science. This means it has practical value and not just research value. Forensic science is defined as the application of the natural sciences (such as biology and chemistry) to the law. Forensic scientists mainly look at physical evidence: they collect it, interpret it, and then draw conclusions from it.

Physical evidence should be the basis for any investigation of a crime. It can be used to establish where a crime occurred, what happened, and, in some cases, who was involved. Physical evidence is the basis for all investigations, and it is the only real account of what has actually happened.

ON THE CASE:

WHAT WOULD HITLER DO?

During the early years of World War II, Germany's armies controlled most of Europe. Military and government officials from the allied countries (the UK, USA, France and the Soviet Union) wanted to know what kinds of events would influence certain enemy leaders. They especially wanted to know what Adolf Hitler, Nazi Germany's dictator, would do.

What would happen if the tide turned and Germany began to lose more and more battles?

What would Hitler be likely to do?

If he were captured, what would be the best way of questioning him about the crimes he committed during the war?

Chief of these crimes were those of the Holocaust: the planning, approving, and carrying out of the slaughter of six million Jewish men, women, and children, as well as millions of other Europeans.

Dr. Walter Langer was a psychiatrist who compiled a psychological assessment of Adolf Hitler. He based his assessment on Hitler's many speeches and a book Hitler had written called *Mein Kampf (My Struggle)*. Langer also used information from interviews with people who had known Hitler personally.

Langer then analysed the information he had collected and was able to produce an assessment of Hitler's most likely behaviour if the war went bad for the German Army.

PROFILING HITLER

Langer suggested eight things as possible scenarios: Hitler might die of natural causes; he might escape to another country; he might be killed in battle; he might be assassinated; he could become mentally ill; there might be a military revolt in which his own armies would turn against him; he might be captured by the enemy; and finally he might commit suicide.

Dr. Langer thought the last scenario was the most likely and his assessment proved to be accurate. As Germany was losing the final battles of World War II, Adolf Hitler killed himself rather than fall into the hands of his enemies.

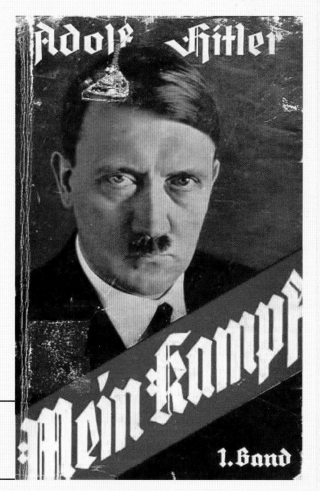

Hitler's *Mein Kampf* became the 'bible' of National Socialism (Nazism) in Germany. The book was published in two volumes in 1925 and 1927, and by 1939, it had sold over 5 million copies and had been translated into 11 languages.

What facts of the crime can this gun tell investigators? If a bullet has been recovered from the body of a murder victim, the bullet can be examined by a firearms expert and matched to the gun that fired it. Therefore, a gun can tell investigators whether or not it was the murder weapon.

Physical evidence is defined as any item (such as a weapon) or substance (such as blood) found at a crime scene that can identify an offender, the facts of the crime, or anything else important to the case. Physical evidence can be absolutely anything: a cigarette butt, a shoe, or a piece of furniture. It can be something left at the crime scene by the people involved, something taken away by them, or something created by them. Early forensic scientists focused not only on the physical evidence, but also on what that could tell investigators about the offender.

Forensic science & profiling

Hans Gross was one of the first forensic scientists to study the criminal and his methods. Gross is thought to be not only one of the founders of forensic science, but also a founder of criminal profiling. In his book *Criminal Psychology*, Gross explored how the best way to understand criminals is to study their crimes.

Edmond Locard was another important figure in the history of forensic science. In 1910, Locard asked the police service for two rooms and two lab assistants to set up a crime laboratory in Lyon in France. Locard was very interested in the way that criminals leave evidence behind at a crime scene and take evidence away with them from the scene.

From this idea he developed 'Locard's Exchange Principle' which is explained in Chapter 4.

In the 1900s, Paul Kirk, an American micro-chemist, who many people consider to be the father of modern forensic science, made a number of contributions to the modern field of criminal profiling. In fact, Kirk was able to examine physical evidence from a crime and then give profile information about the offender based on that evidence. In one case involving a glove left at the scene of a burglary, Kirk said the criminal:

- Was a labourer in construction
- Was mostly involved in pushing a wheelbarrow
- Lived outside of the town on a small farm
- Was southern European
- Raised chickens and kept a cow or a horse

Kirk's profile was based on the physical evidence left behind by the criminal that had been examined in a laboratory. After the criminal was caught, all of the above characteristics turned out to be true except for the second one – he drove a tractor rather than pushing a wheelbarrow!

One of the biggest ways in which forensic science can help profiling comes from crime

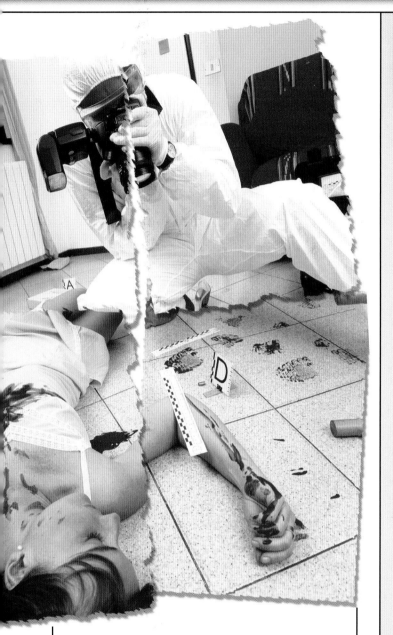

A murder crime scene has been set up as part of a training exercise for crime scene investigators (C.S.I.s). If this were a real murder scene, the photographs of the corpse, the position of the body, and the bloody footprints on the floor would all be parts of the jigsaw puzzle that the criminal profiler tries to put together when reconstructing the crime.

A CAREER IN CRIMINAL PROFILING
HOWARD TETEN OF THE FBI

In 1970, an FBI special agent called Howard Teten began teaching a criminal profiling course called 'Applied Criminology' at the FBI National Academy. In the 1960s, while serving as a law enforcement officer in California, Teten had studied with Dr. Paul Kirk (the renowned forensic scientist) and other forensics experts, and had developed investigation skills and ideas that could be used in profiling criminals. Working with a New York FBI agent, Pat Mullany, Teten taught profiling techniques across the USA: how to dissect a crime, understanding abnormal behaviours, and how to see those behaviours using evidence found at a crime scene.

During the 1970s, Teten and Mullany successfully used their profiling skills during major hostage negotiations, and their techniques were soon being taught to FBI hostage negotiators.

In 1972, an FBI agent named Jack Kirsch started the FBI's Behavioral Science Unit (BSU). He allowed Teten and Mullany to work on profiles and profiling research, furthering the understanding of this area of forensic investigation. The work of Teten, Mullany and Kirsch made a huge contribution to the world of criminal profiling.

reconstruction. Having the physical evidence is one thing, but having it can only tell you so much. To be able to figure out what happened in a crime you need someone to put the evidence together in the same way you put a jigsaw together from the pieces.

Crime reconstruction involves figuring out the actions of various people involved in the crime. A crime reconstruction may be able to tell you whether someone was standing or sitting when they received an injury, where one person was in relation to another person when the crime happened, or what was moved or changed during the crime.

Information from a reconstruction can be useful to investigators, and it can be used in court to help explain to a jury what happened during a crime.

How to reconstruct a crime scene

There are many different ways to reconstruct a crime. Some profilers say it should be done like a story; others say it should be put together like the scenes in a film; some profilers say that the evidence should be laid out and rearranged to come up with ideas about how things might have happened until you are left with the only possibility that makes sense.

To be able to properly reconstruct a crime you have to understand evidence and its importance within crime. Blood can be used not only to tell you where people were when they started to bleed, but also whether they were more likely to be standing or sitting, what happened after they started to bleed, and also who it was that was bleeding. Evidence from a crime can be used in a reconstruction to find out the direction someone moved in; how long something happened for; where it happened; or to find out what happened first, last or any time in between.

Some of this same evidence may be sent off to the crime lab to be analysed for other key pieces of information. In the case of a blood sample, this would be to figure out who the blood belongs to. A gun might be sent to the lab to find out whether the bullet that killed a victim was shot from that actual weapon.

A badly injured robbery victim crawls to a glass door and desperately tries to get help. When the police arrive, the victim is lying on the floor – dead. However, the bloody handprint on the door will show investigators what the victim did after they were attacked, but before they died.

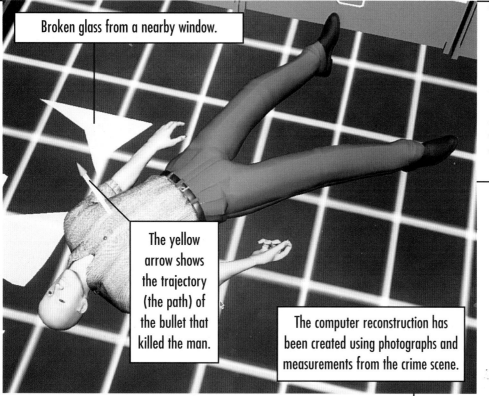

Broken glass from a nearby window.

Three-dimensional (3D) computer models can be used to reconstruct a crime scene. This reconstruction could help a profiler work out what happened during the crime, for example where was the killer standing when they shot the man?

The yellow arrow shows the trajectory (the path) of the bullet that killed the man.

The computer reconstruction has been created using photographs and measurements from the crime scene.

Seeing the scene

Visiting the crime scene is important for a profiler doing a reconstruction. Some crime scenes have hundreds of photographs taken of them and hours of video tape, but until they see the actual scene, a profiler might not be able to get a real idea of the layout of the crime scene, for example, the size of the room, or the distance between objects in the room.

No matter how well a crime is documented, when preparing a reconstruction nothing beats standing in the place where the crime took place!

WHAT DOES IT TAKE TO BECOME A PROFILER?

Some profilers are part of a police force or other government agency, such as the FBI, in the USA. Others work privately.

Profiling is not a single discipline, but involves a set of skills that are developed through study and practice in other areas.

These include:

• Psychology

• Criminology

• Forensic Science

• Investigation

In addition, a number of skills and qualities are of use to the profiler in their assessment of crimes. These include:

• Critical thinking (being able to develop an idea or concept, and analyse and evaluate information gathered from observation, experience, reflection or reason)

• Analytical skills

• Energy and determination

• Integrity and ethics

• Knowledge in a number of subjects, such as criminal investigation, psychology and criminology

ON THE CASE:

THE MAD BOMBER OF NEW YORK

In the late 1940s and early 1950s, someone was setting off homemade bombs throughout New York City. At first the bombs were very simple: pipe bombs made from cut pieces of metal pipe packed with explosives. Sometimes the bombs even failed to detonate (explode). Eventually, though, the bombs became bigger and more powerful.

In 1956, a bomb exploded in a cinema, injuring a number of people. No one had been killed...this time! Desperate to find the person the newspapers were calling the 'Mad Bomber of New York', detectives were willing to try something different.

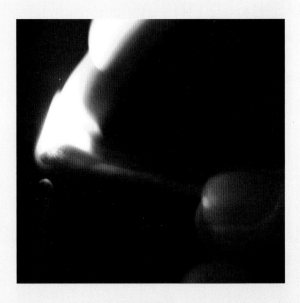

PROFILING THE MAD BOMBER

Dr. James Brussel was a criminal psychiatrist. He worked with people whose mental illnesses led them to commit crimes. Dr. Brussel looked carefully at the evidence details and letters sent by the bomber to the police department and the media. He told the police the bomber was:

- A single, white, heavily built, middle-aged man.
- He had a grudge against the utility company Con Edison, and was possibly a former employee who had suffered some injury at work – hence the grudge.
- He was likely to be a Roman Catholic.
- The man would have been born in a foreign country although he might now be a U.S. citizen. He did not live in the state of New York but probably in a nearby state, such as Connecticut.
- The bomber probably lived with female relatives.
- He would most likely wear a double-breasted suit.

Detectives weren't sure whether they should believe all this. How would Dr. Brussel know these things, especially something like the type of suit the bomber would wear? Dr. Brussel explained his conclusions were based on careful observation.

- The bomber would most likely be male because all the other bombing crimes that had happened in recent history had been committed by males.
- The wording of the bomber's letters seemed to point to a person for whom English was a second language.
- The bomber used old-fashioned phrases in his letters that were not used much anymore. However, the grammar and spelling were correct and pointed to a person with a high-school education. English may not have been the bomber's native language, but he was comfortable using it.
- In the 1940s and 1950s, most of the immigrants coming to the United States were from countries close to the Baltic Sea such as Poland, Latvia, Estonia and Lithuania.
- The fact that bombs were the chosen weapon pointed to a person who came from a culture that would see a bomb as a weapon, and homemade bombs were often the weapon of choice in the Baltic area.
- Most people from the Baltic area were Roman Catholic.
- And the suit? The double-breasted suit was popular at the time and would likely be worn by a single, white, middle-aged man.

FINDING THE MAD BOMBER

Drawing on his knowledge and experience of different types of mental illness, Dr. Brussel concluded the bomber showed some personality traits that fitted with a mental illness called paranoia. A person suffering from paranoia would be likely to think that other people had something against them when, in fact, this wasn't the case.

So...the police now had Dr. Brussel's very detailed profile, but how could they use it to find the bomber?

Dr. Brussel suggested that the profile details be published in the newspapers! He felt that the bomber's paranoia was such that he would respond in some way to the information in the profile. At the same time, clerks at Con Edison began the monumental task of examining all their old employee records to find out if any ex-employees fitted the profile. A possible suspect soon came to light. And when, as Dr. Brussel had

Under arrest! George Metesky, wearing a double-breasted suit, is escorted by police officers and detectives.

predicted, the bomber made contact in response to seeing his profile in the media, the bomber gave away further clues to his identity that matched up with the employee record uncovered at Con Edison!

A SMARTLY-DRESSED BOMBER

The suspect's name was George Metesky, and English was indeed his second language. When the police arrived at his home to arrest him, Metesky had to change out of his bathrobe. He reappeared after changing into a double-breasted suit!

Metesky went to trial and was convicted of attempted murder and bombing. He was also judged to be insane. Instead of prison, he was sent to a mental hospital for insane criminals and held there until 1973 when he was released. Metesky returned home to Connecticut and lived there until his death in 1994.

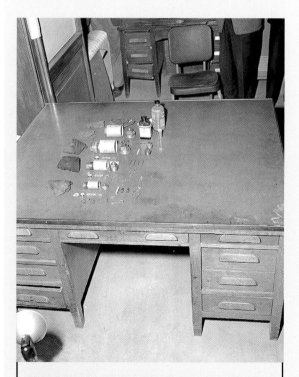

The ingredients for making bombs are displayed on a table at police headquarters. The evidence was collected from the home of George Metesky after his arrest in 1957.

Profiling inputs: a crime scene photograph. Spots of blood from the victim's kitchen. Tests in the crime lab confirm it is the victim's blood.

One of the most important goals of a good profile is to narrow down the suspect pool so detectives can focus their investigation. There are many different types of criminal profiling, but most are based on three main methods that are used around the world.

The three methods are *Criminal Investigative Analysis (C.I.A.)* practiced by the FBI and people trained by the FBI. *Investigative Psychology (I.P.)* developed by David Canter in the UK, and the most recent method to be developed which is called *Behavioural Evidence Analysis (B.E.A.)*. This method was developed by profiler Brent Turvey in the USA.

Many police agencies and private profilers around the world follow the FBI's *C.I.A.* method which includes the similarity of the current crime to past crimes as part of the profile.

Criminal Investigative Analysis

A *C.I.A.* profiler will draw on their own experience, that of their colleagues, studies conducted by the FBI and other information available about the type of crime that has been committed.

An initial assessment of the crime is also made by looking at the crime scene information such as photographs and videos, police reports, eyewitness and victim statements, and autopsy reports.

In the 1980s, the FBI stated there were six steps involved in the *C.I.A.* profiling process.

The first step is called 'Profiling Inputs'. This is where all of the above information about the crime is assessed. This also includes a study of

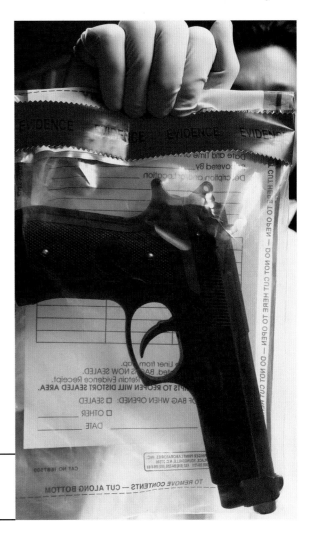

Profiling inputs: a 'bagged and tagged' gun found in the victim's garden. Firearms experts have matched the bullet that killed the victim to this gun.

the victim of the crime: their age, height, weight, personal habits, hobbies, health, employment, friends and family, fears, and just about anything else that may be important. This information can not only show why the victim was chosen, but also their risk of becoming a victim of this type of crime; what the offender was willing to do to get them; and the offender's skill at committing the crime.

The second step, 'Decision Process Models', places all of the information collected during the 'Profiling Inputs' step into behavioural patterns. This second step looks at whether there is more than one victim and, if the crime is a murder, what type of murder it is. 'Decision Process Models' also looks at the intent of the offender – did they mean to commit this crime, or was it an accident that happened during the carrying out of another type of crime. For example, did the offender kill a homeowner who disturbed them while they were carrying out a robbery. Victim and offender risk are also important here. Victim risk refers to the risk the victim is at because of their job, personality, habits and hobbies. Offender risk is the risk the offender takes to get a certain victim at a certain time.

Profiling inputs: a witness statement. An eyewitness report states that the victim was seen jogging in the park at 5:00 p.m. on Friday afternoon.

Profiling inputs: an autopsy report. The forensic pathologist confirms that the 'manner of death' was murder. The 'cause of death' was a single gunshot wound to the head. The time of death was some time between 6:00 p.m. and 10:00 p.m. on Friday evening.

EVIDENCE

Profiling inputs: 'bagged and tagged' bullets. This evidence was found in a litter bin at the park. They are the correct calibre (size) for the gun found in the victim's garden.

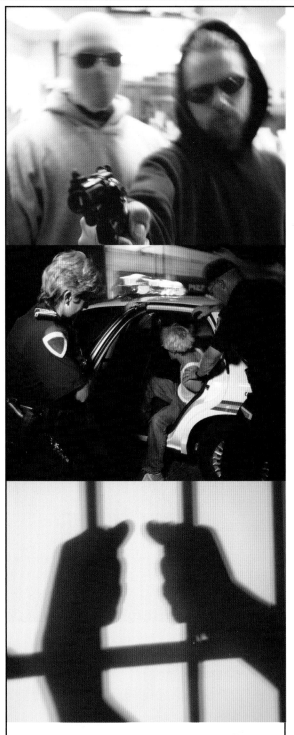

A violent robber is becoming more extreme in the treatment of his victims. A profile is prepared and given to the investigators. The suspect pool is narrowed to one man, and the law enforcement officers apprehend the suspect. The profile has saved time and might just have saved the life of the robber's next victim!

'Crime Assessment' is the third stage. This looks at the sequence of events of both the offender and the victim. This can tell the profiler how organised the offender is, how they selected the victim, whether there is any staging (this is when an offender changes evidence to throw investigators off track), and the criminal's motivation.

Stage four is the actual 'Criminal Profile' describing the type of person who committed the offence. This would include physical descriptions, physical characteristics, habits, beliefs, personality, and the offender's behaviour before, during and after the crime.

Stages five and six involve 'Investigation' and 'Apprehension'. Investigation comes after the profile is given. The suspect pool is narrowed down and all the current suspects are assessed. Apprehension involves arresting and prosecuting the main suspect and then comparing the suspect to the features in the profile to see how well they match. If they do not match, the profile is looked at to see why.

In the mid 1990s, the FBI profiler Roy Hazelwood changed the number of steps involved to only three. The first of these later steps is 'Determine Offender Behaviour'. This is because it is the offender's behaviour that serves as the basis for the profile. This information can come either from the physical evidence of the crime, or from the victim's story of what happened, if the victim is still alive.

The second step is 'Analyse the Behaviour', where the profiler looks at the verbal, sexual and physical behaviour of the offender to try and find the reason the crime was committed.

The last step is the actual profile that gives the characteristics of the offender.

Investigative Psychology

In 1985, police from Scotland Yard in London, asked David Canter, a lecturer in psychology from the University of Surrey, to help find a murderer. Canter was asked whether or not the theory of psychology could be applied to a criminal investigation to help the police focus their search for a man the media called 'The Railway Rapist'.

From his work on this case, Canter developed a whole field of psychology that has come to be known as *Investigative Psychology*. Canter uses a number of theories to produce a profile. Like the FBI, Canter's method is based on looking at the similarities of this crime to past crimes of the same type.

Investigative Psychology uses something called 'the five factor model'. This describes the way the offender interacted with the victim, the type of crime committed, the time and the place it was committed and the criminal's skill and knowledge of police procedures.

Factor one is called 'Interpersonal Coherence'. It assumes that criminals will behave the same way during their crimes as they do with other people in their daily lives. This means that a generally angry person in their day-to-day lives will be generally angry when dealing with their victims.

Psychologists discovered many years ago that a person whose personality leads them to behave violently to people in their everyday lives, such as family members, is likely to behave violently to their victims during a crime. This theory forms the 'Interpersonal Coherence' stage of David Canter's profiling method.

A dark, deserted street in the middle of the night. Why wait here? Does the criminal know this area? Does he know someone who lives on this street? Is he waiting for someone to come by? What is the significance of the late hour (the time) and this street (the place) to this criminal?

The second factor is 'Significance of Time and Place'. This argues that both the location of the crime and the time it was committed are important. It asks the question, "Does the time and place of the crime say anything about the criminal?" For example, a crime committed in the middle of the day may suggest that an offender doesn't have a job. A crime committed in a remote location that is difficult to get to, may suggest that the offender is familiar with the area and had access to a car to drive to the crime scene. Time and place may suggest a connection between the offender and the victim, the offender and the location, or the victim and the location.

'Criminal Characteristics', the third factor, assumes that criminals who commit similar crimes have similar characteristics. It also helps the profiler understand the type of crime they are dealing with and to distinguish between different types of crimes.

'Criminal Career', the fourth factor, and 'Forensic Awareness', the fifth, are similar. During a criminal career, an offender will learn and change their behaviour. They may learn that an eyewitness description can be published in the media to help the public identify them (not good for the criminal if they want to stay free) so they start wearing clothes that stops a victim from being able to identify them.

'Forensic Awareness' is specifically about the knowledge an offender has of police and scientific tactics. This may include cleaning blood from their clothes or wiping away fingerprints.

Behavioural Evidence Analysis

Behavioural Evidence Analysis, or *B.E.A.*, was developed by Brent Turvey, a forensic scientist and criminal profiler in private practice in the United States. Working in private practice means that Turvey works cases and develops profiles, but does not work for a particular law enforcement agency. As a student, Turvey interviewed convicted sex offenders and serial killers to try and better understand what they did and why. The *B.E.A.* method relies on the forensic evidence of a particular crime, and not research in general. This means specific conclusions about specific cases can be reached.

Criminal career factor: the victims say the man who robbed them had dark brown hair. The robber lies low for a while, but he will not make the same mistake again. When he robs his next victim he wears a ski mask. Forensic awareness factor: the criminal learned long ago to wear gloves to avoid leaving prints at the scene.

Evidence is everything

In 1991, while studying psychology, Turvey was interviewing Jerome Brudos, a serial murderer in prison. Before actually talking to Brudos, Turvey had spent a considerable amount of time studying the crime reports, court records and physical evidence. During the interview, Brudos lied about almost everything. He argued that he hadn't done some of the crimes even though the evidence against him included photographs he had taken of his victims in which he had accidentally included himself! It occurred to Turvey that offenders have a

In 2000, a British doctor named Dr. Harold Shipman was convicted of murdering 15 of his patients by administering lethal doses of diamorphine. An official report into the case concluded that it was likely Shipman killed between 215 and 260 people over a period of 23 years. The 'Victimology' of Shipman's murdered patients would show the majority were middle-aged or elderly women, who all lived in the same area of Hyde, Greater Manchester.

reason to lie, and because of this, the only true record of what happened in a crime is the physical evidence.

When constructing a *B.E.A.* profile, all suspect, victim and witness statements are treated as theories only, not as solid proof. Only when a statement has been compared to the physical evidence and that evidence either confirms or denies the witness statement, will it be relied on as evidence that can be used for the profile. The *B.E.A.* method has four basic steps.

The 'Equivocal Forensic Analysis' is the first step. This says that all evidence has more than one meaning (which is the definition of equivocal) and that its true meaning cannot be understood until everything has been examined in context. This stage assesses the physical evidence, and like other profiling approaches this can include virtually anything such as crime scene photos and videos,

police reports, autopsy reports and witness and victim statements. It is during this stage that a complete crime reconstruction will be done. The crime reconstruction is an assessment of the criminal's behaviour during the crime and the sequence in which things happened.

Victimology

Next, 'Victimology' examines all aspects of the victim including their physical characteristics such as height, weight, age and sex as well as their habits and hobbies, job, friends and family. The victimology stage is pretty much a profile of the victim and as much time should be spent trying to understand the victim as the profiler spends trying to understand the criminal. The victimology also looks at the risk of the victim of becoming the target of certain types of crime.

Let's say you have a victim who has an unpredictable routine, travels different ways to work, works their own hours, has a reliable vehicle in good condition, doesn't use drugs and alcohol, and is naturally a very cautious person. This victim would be described as low risk because of all of these things. One day, because of construction work on a local road, the victim is forced to take a detour to get home along a road that is in bad condition with little lighting. While driving they get a flat tyre so they stop to change the wheel. While they are doing this, they are attacked.

A young woman has been attacked. What's the 'Victimology'? The victim is a woman aged 25 years; she attends exercise classes on a Tuesday night between 7:00 p.m. and 9:00 p.m; she lives alone in a house on the beach; after the exercise class she walks home alone, along the beach.

One theory we might have is that the attack is because of this opportunity (they were simply in the wrong place at the wrong time), and this is supported by them not only having an unpredictable routine, but also because their behaviour on this night was unpredictable due to the detour. It's a good theory, but it would need to be checked against physical evidence from the crime: for example, looking into the background of the victim to see whether they were being harassed by someone. Perhaps they might have told a friend they were being followed each night on the way home. If this was the case, the random attack theory would be in doubt.

Crime scene characteristics

'Crime Scene Characteristics' is the third stage. These are the important features of a crime scene that show decisions made by the criminal about the victim and the location of the crime. The profiler develops ideas about the meaning of certain things to the offender. If the offender attacks someone in one location (this is called the primary crime scene) and then moves their body somewhere else to dispose of it (called the disposal site) the choice of location for the attack and the disposal might show some knowledge of these locations. For example, if the disposal site is remote and far away from places people normally go, how did the offender know about it? What normally happens in this location? How would the offender know about it? How did the offender know they wouldn't be disturbed or seen?

CRIME SCENE CHARACTERISTICS

Crime Scene Characteristics include the following information:

- Crime location and crime scene type (where the victim was met by the offender, where they were attacked, where they were left etc).
- The offender's approach to the victim.
- The offender's style of attack of the victim.

- The use of weapons.
- The victim's resistance.
- Items taken by the offender.
- Items left behind.
- The criminal's motivation.

Once these first three stages have been worked through, it is possible to provide a number of characteristics about the offender in the form of a profile. This is referred to as the 'Offender Characteristics' stage and involves looking for behavioural patterns.

Offender characteristics

The profiler should define the particular characteristic (for example, a criminal skill) and then show the evidence of that characteristic in the crime (such as the ability to pick a lock or climb a building). Some of the characteristics that might be found in a *B.E.A.* profile can be seen in the table (right).

Inductive and deductive profiling

Though there are different profiling methods, most rely on the same information to produce a profile and many methods even agree on the types of things that you can tell about an offender.

Where the methods are most different is in the type of logic they use in arguing for the characteristics they give in a profile.

Logic is the science of making an argument and in profiling there are two important types.

If an offender has picked a lock in order to commit a crime, a profiler would suggest they had a history of criminal behaviour. They might already have a criminal record, and this could help identify them.

The average characteristics of offenders carrying out a particular type of crime are used in inductive profiling. If in past cases of a particular type of crime the perpetrator has been a white, European male, the conclusion is that a new case involving the same type of crime, is likely to have a white, European male perpetrator.

Inductive profiling

The first type of logic is induction. This is a statistical method that believes research on past offenders can be used to provide averaged offender 'types' which can be applied to the current case. An assessment is made about the degree of similarity between a current case (say a murder) and past cases of the same or similar type (other murders, drawn from research, studies, or the profiler's past experience). If in the cases from the past, the average characteristics of the offenders were that they were usually between 18 and 25 years of age, male, and the same race as the victim, then this would be given as the profile in the current case. The FBI's *Criminal Investigative Analysis* method and David Canter's *Investigative Psychology* are both examples of inductive profiling.

Induction gives conclusions based on probability: if the offender is the same as past offenders, they probably have this set of characteristics.

OFFENDER CHARACTERISTICS

The offender characteristics that can be found in a *B.E.A.* profile include:

- Knowledge of the victim.
- Knowledge of the crime scene.
- Evidence of criminal skill.

- Specialist knowledge of certain methods and materials (such as tying a knot in a certain way, or flying a helicopter).
- Evidence of criminal history.
- State of mind (such as the offender's emotional state during the crime).

Deductive profiling

The second style of reasoning is deductive. This is a much more involved and detailed process. It involves the collection and interpretation of a wide range of evidence, in which the meaning of that evidence is established with certainty (remember, this is the purpose of the 'Equivocal Forensic Analysis' stage in *B.E.A.*). The deductive approach takes evidence, finds out what theories it may represent and then tests the theories against the evidence. Any theory that cannot be supported by the evidence is ruled out. Ideally, this leads the profiler to one logical conclusion that is supported by the evidence. An example of this would be a criminal who called the victim by name during the crime. Unless they looked at the victim's driving licence or something else with the victim's name on it; or unless they asked the victim their name during the offence, we can say with certainty that the offender knew the victim, or at least knew of them.

Probabilities & certainties

While induction is based on probability, it may even be more probable than not, deduction is certain. What this means is that if the evidence is true and accurate and its interpretation is also accurate, then the conclusion drawn from that must also be true and accurate. To be able to give this level of certainty, deduction uses the scientific method, which means getting knowledge through collecting and testing of evidence, called experimentation. Another way to think about deductive profiling would be 'evidence based' because it is guided by the physical and behavioural evidence and doesn't consider general types and average offenders.

Deductive profiling uses the scientific method: observation – searching for and documenting evidence; hypothesis – considering what the evidence might mean; experimentation – testing the evidence to see if the hypothesis is right or wrong; data collection – carefully recording the test results; conclusion – using the evidence facts, and only the facts, as part of the profile.

INDUCTIVE AND DEDUCTIVE IN ACTION

Below are two examples of profile characteristics that were given in real criminal profiles. The first is inductive and you can see the way the conclusion is based on what is generally known about crimes of this type. The second is deductive and you can see the way the conclusion is drawn only from the evidence in the current case.

INDUCTIVE PROFILE CHARACTERISTIC

KIDNAP CASE

Characteristic:

It is likely the kidnapper is male and of white European racial extraction.

Conclusion

This conclusion is based on the fact that most kidnappers abduct people of their own race and in this case the victim is white European. This conclusion is based on other similar crimes where the victim was the same race as their kidnapper.

DEDUCTIVE PROFILE CHARACTERISTIC

STALKING CASE

Characteristic:

The offender has extensive knowledge of the victim's home (the crime scene).

Conclusion

This conclusion is based on e-mails (evidence) sent to the victim in which the stalker showed a detailed knowledge of the layout of the victim's house. He knew the location of the victim's bedroom because he went straight to her room and did not go into any other rooms in the house. This conclusion is not based on any other crimes, but specific evidence (the emails) that relate to this case only.

A Crime Scene Investigator (C.S.I.) removes a tiny fragment of fibre from a broken window. The fibre will be analysed in a crime lab and it might be possible to find out what type of garment it came from. Knowledge of the type of garment worn by the perpetrator could be useful to a profiler.

During a robbery, an offender pulls a victim's shirt up over her head. Was this done to stop the victim seeing the robber? Did the offender do it to increase the fear in the victim or to stop the victim struggling? If a robber takes something from a victim, was it to keep as a souvenir so they could later relive their crimes, or did they take it to sell for money?

All of the things a profiler does and the interpretation of the above behaviours rely on a number of practices, many of which have been used for a long time in other areas of forensic science and criminal investigation. This chapter will provide an overview of these practices.

Locard's Exchange Principle

'Locard's Exchange Principle' is named after Edmond Locard, who set up the world's first crime lab in Lyon, France. 'Locard's Exchange Principle' is one of the most fundamental in forensic science, crime investigation and criminal profiling. It says that when an offender enters a crime scene they take something of that scene away with them and leave something of themselves behind.

For example, an offender who breaks a window to get access to a house may carry away fragments of glass from the window on his hands or clothing. If the offender cuts himself he will also leave blood on the broken glass, and maybe even leave some torn pieces of his clothes. When he enters the house, he tracks dirt from the backyard into the house where he searches for cash and valuables, leaving some traces of

Locard's Exchange Principle says that not only has this bootprint been left at the crime scene, but material from the scene is likely to have been taken away on the boot.

blood on the furniture. While he is walking through the house he picks up some carpet fibres on his shoes and takes them back to his own house. All of this transfer between the crime scene and the offender is because of 'Locard's Exchange Principle'.

The Modus Operandi

A criminal's MO (*Modus Operandi*, or Method of Operation) refers to those things the criminal had to do to successfully complete the crime. The *modus operandi* is functional, that means it serves some purpose and doesn't have a psychological meaning to the criminal. The MO is usually aimed at one of the following three things:

- To ensure the criminal's success

- To protect the criminal's identity

- To help with the criminal's escape

The elements in a crime that can be classified as MO related are almost endless and depend in part on the type of crime and its individual features. Some of the things that are related to MO can be seen in the table on this page.

A CRIMINAL'S MO

The following things could be related to a criminal's MO during a crime. They are all things that aim at making the crime a success.

- The use of gloves and a ski mask conceals the criminal's identity).
- The use of a weapon (subdues the victim).
- Use of ropes or tape (stops the victim escaping).
- Stealing a getaway car (helps the criminal to escape).

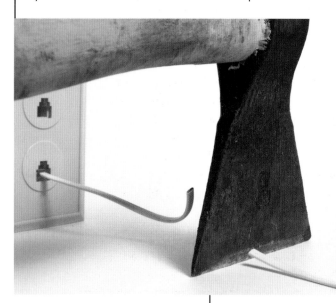

As part of a criminal's MO, the cutting of a telephone wire ensured the criminal was able to get away from the crime scene before the victim could summon help.

The MO can be affected by opportunity, by the criminal being interrupted during the offence, or by the reaction of the victim to the crime, such as struggling or fighting off the attacker. The MO can also change owing to experience: a criminal will learn things as they commit more crimes and will use those things to help them get away with other crimes.

Signature

The MO refers to functional aspects of the crime, but the signature refers to those things the offender did that they didn't have to do. The signature is not a functional aspect. It shows a physical or psychological need that the offender has.

Signature is broken into two individual components, or parts. This is quite a tricky concept, but it works like this: the first part is signature behaviour. This refers to the individual behaviours that make up the signature act. The second part is signature aspect.

An offender behaves violently towards his victim. He attacks her then ties her up and covers her mouth with tape.

This refers to the theme of the behaviours. Let's take an example: if an offender gets a victim to read them a script telling them how important and powerful they are, reading the script would be the signature behaviour. The signature aspect would be the offender's psychological need to hear the kidnap victim tell them how important they are.

While the MO may be useful in some cases for linking the crimes of a serial offender, MOs are often too general or too common to be useful for this purpose.

Signature on the other hand, is more individual to each offender. The idea is this: each of us goes through an individual range of developmental issues as we grow up. The family that raises us, the places that we live in, and our culture provides us all with a relatively unique set of experiences and beliefs that make us who we are. Because criminal behaviour is an extension of our everyday behaviour, these same experiences and beliefs influence not only how we are with our friends, families and co-workers, but also the way a criminal will interact with a victim. Our unique experiences

An offender who is violent towards his victim is likely to behave in the same way to the people in his everyday life.

shape our behaviour and cause criminals to have certain signature behaviours. These signatures can be seen by a profiler.

The example we looked at in an earlier chapter is good here, too. A person who is generally angry with those around them will also act angrily towards a victim during a crime. The basic idea here is simple: behaviour reflects personality and so we examine the behaviour to understand the personality.

If an offender gets angry with a victim because the victim tries to escape (which would mess up the offender's plans) then this would be an MO because frightening the victim will help the offender to carry out the crime. An offender who gets angry when he doesn't have to, is showing signature behaviour. He has a physical or psychological need to be angry with his victim.

The things that happen to us as we grow up and develop give us all a unique set of experiences. Being bullied as a child, or being the bully are, for example, just two experiences that will influence our personalities as we grow older.

37

A huge stack of cash stolen from a bank! The motive? You've got it – profit!

Another feature of an offence that it may be useful for a profiler to establish is the motive. It is through understanding the signature that we better understand the motive in an offence.

If the offender is angry with the victim during the crime, even when the victim is doing what they are told and there is no need for the offender to be angry, this is the offender's signature. In terms of motive, this would be what a profiler calls an anger motivated offence. Motives can be used to identify suspect pools. Therefore, establishing motives can be an important part of putting together a profile.

Motive

There are six general motives for most crimes. A criminal may show only one motive through their behaviour, or they may show a mixture of motives in the same offence or over a number of different offences. The six motives are:

Power Reassurance: These criminals have low self esteem and commit crimes to make them feel better about themselves. These criminals aren't usually violent, and they may even try to get the victim involved in the offence, such as talking to them like a friend.

An offender sets fire to a building to cover up a murder. The motive behind this case of arson would be 'crime concealment'. But if an offender were to set fire to the workplace he had just been fired from, this would be 'anger retaliatory' – revenge!

Power Assertive: These criminals also have low self esteem and also commit crimes to make themselves feel better. However, unlike the 'Reassurance Oriented' offender (in the first example), they aren't interested in getting the victim involved. These criminals make themselves feel better by making other people feel worse! These offenders are more likely to be violent.

Anger Retaliatory:

These criminals are out for revenge. They feel they are putting something right that may actually be real, or it may be something they have imagined. By committing the offence, they feel they are getting payback!

Anger Excitation:

These offenders are also angry, and because of this are very likely to be violent. Their offences may last a long time and they are more likely to keep a record, such as a video or photographs, of their crimes. These offenders get a great amount of satisfaction out of the suffering they put their victims through.

Profit: These crime are simple! The criminal wants money so they commit a crime to get it. They either steal cash, or something they can sell for cash.

Crime Concealment:

This is more of a secondary motive. This means it usually requires some other crime to have happened, and this crime will have a motive all of its own. We might have an 'Anger Retaliatory' offender who kills a family member, but who then sets the house on fire to hide the original murder. The motive for the arson crime would be crime concealment.

1) A murderer points his gun at his victim. The motive for his crime – power assertion: to hurt someone and make them suffer.

2) A robber points his gun at the attendant in a gas station and tells him to empty the cash register. The motive for this crime – profit. However, if the robber shoots the attendant to stop him dialling 999, the motive behind this new crime is concealment.

Staging

Sometimes criminals do things to throw the investigation off track. They might clean up, or move furniture around so the crime scene looks different to when the crime actually happened. They may throw things around to make investigators and profilers believe there was a struggle when there wasn't.

One of the first things a profiler must consider is whether the evidence at a crime scene is an accurate reflection of the way the crime happened, or whether someone has done something to change the appearance of the crime. If the evidence has been changed, this may change the profiler's opinion about what happened. If it has been changed, it is very important to find out how the evidence is now, how it has been changed, and how it was before.

When a criminal alters the evidence in a crime on purpose, this is called 'staging'. For example, if a family member kills another family member but wants to claim it was an intruder who broke in, they may smash a window, move furniture around, and take away items such as money or jewellery to help their claim it was a burglary that went wrong.

To detect staging, the profiler should do a complete crime reconstruction to see what evidence there is, what has been changed, how it has been changed, and how those items of evidence should look. If the evidence doesn't look as it should, it might mean the crime has been staged.

There's one odd thing about staging, though, that profilers always need to remember: staging is almost always done by the most likely suspect in the crime. So if a profiler sees staging, they need to consider who has the most to gain by making the crime appear this way!

Context is everything

The context of an act relates to the set of circumstances or facts around that act.

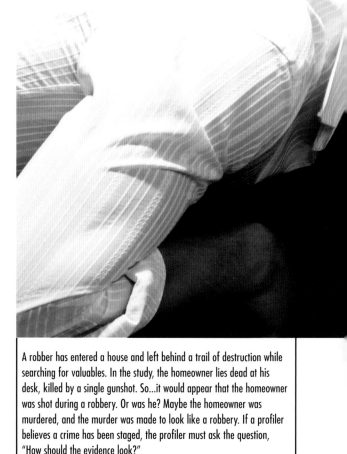

A robber has entered a house and left behind a trail of destruction while searching for valuables. In the study, the homeowner lies dead at his desk, killed by a single gunshot. So...it would appear that the homeowner was shot during a robbery. Or was he? Maybe the homeowner was murdered, and the murder was made to look like a robbery. If a profiler believes a crime has been staged, the profiler must ask the question, "How should the evidence look?"

When examining the behaviour of a criminal during a crime, the context in which the crime occurred is important if you want to understand the real nature of the crime.

A profiler should never take a single piece of information and draw a conclusion from it without understanding the context of the behaviour. An example of a behaviour and how a profiler might question its context is shown on page 41.

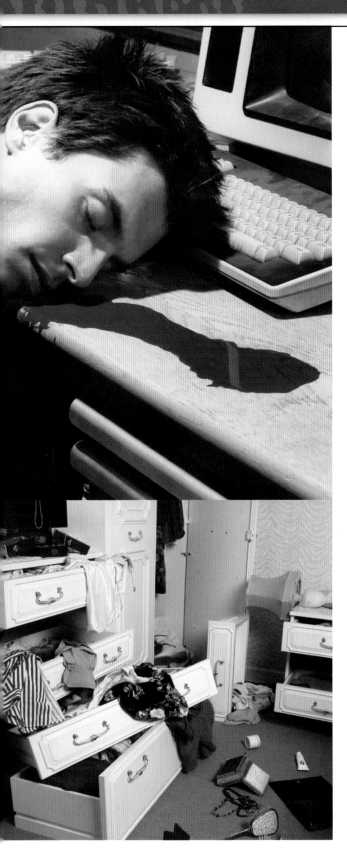

CRIMINAL ACTIONS IN CONTEXT

If you remember back to the start of this chapter, we gave an example of offender behaviour: a criminal took something belonging to a victim. To find out what this behaviour could mean, we need to know the context.

So, was the context that the offender took the item from the victim to sell it?

To find out if this was the context, the profiler might ask:

- How much would it be worth to sell?
- Did the offender take a pair of earrings, or only one?
- Was the thing the offender took small and worthless, even though there were other more valuable items in plain sight?

The possible contexts could be:

- If the item is very valuable, it was stolen to be sold.
- If the item wasn't worth anything and was very cheaply made, then it probably means it was taken as a souvenir of the crime.
- If just one earring from a pair was stolen, the context could be that it was taken as a souvenir.

41

The C.S.I.s have recovered all the evidence from the scene of a murder. The forensic pathologist has written an autopsy report and the detectives have interviewed dozens of witnesses. The investigation needs a jumpstart. The detectives decide to call in a criminal profiler.

Some law enforcement agencies have their own profilers. Other times, detectives may hire a private profiler to consult on a case. Detectives make contact with private profilers through the Internet and by email, or they might be put in contact with a profiler by co-workers who have worked with this expert before. Sometimes detectives will read books on profiling to see who is working on particular types of cases and might be able to help them.

Once a detective has found a profiler they usually make personal contact to find out if the profiler can offer them an insight into this particular case.

It isn't all about the detective though, sometimes the profiler might feel they cannot help, or they may believe that the case cannot be profiled.

When detectives and the profiler meet up they will usually discuss the type of case, the people involved, the location of the crime, and just about any other information necessary or known. The detectives will then provide the profiler with information about the case such as victim details, photographs and videos of the crime scene and the evidence, the autopsy report, and statements from witnesses and suspects.

The profiler will then examine the evidence, and may go back to detectives with questions about the evidence, or to ask for more information or details. With all the available evidence in place, the profiler will then begin the work of putting together the profile using the methods we have examined in this book. Finally the profiler produces a written report of their conclusions and meets with the detectives to go through the profile to make sure that the information is understood.

On page 43 you can read a page from a real profile – the original report is nine pages long. Then turn the page for some real life criminal profiling questions.

A profiler meets with detectives to discuss the criminal profile he is preparing for a case.

ON THE CASE:

TRUE LIFE MURDER PROFILE

The FBI's Behavioral Analysis Unit (BAU), working with evidence provided by the Baton Rouge Police Department, in Louisiana, put together this profile on the killer of three women in Baton Rouge, USA.

This excerpt is just one page from the profile that was prepared:

This is an 'impulsive' individual. When determined to do something, he disregards the consequences of his acts. However, his impulsivity should not be confused with lack of planning.

This impulsivity has likely brought him to the attention of law enforcement in the past, even if for seemingly minor offences, including trespassing, breaking and entering, and peeping.

His decision to attack each of the three women when he did may have been spontaneous or impulsive. However, because he had knowledge of the women's schedules and lifestyles, it would have lessened the 'recklessness' of having made a spontaneous decision.

The BAU believes that this offender lost control during the assault of this victim Charlotte Murray Pace. Losing control would have angered him. He does not like losing control, and he would have been noticeably angry and agitated for sometime after the Pace homicide. People around him would have seen this agitation and will recall any disparaging remarks he might have made about Ms. Pace when her homicide was discussed – either by others or in the media. He would have appeared very interested in media reports following the homicide.

If the offender was accountable for his time on the day Pace was murdered, and he had to return to his normal schedule, his distraction would have been very noticeable to others around him. However, if at all possible, he would not have returned to his normal schedule, and his absence from that schedule would have been noted by others.

People who know this offender, know that he hates losing control – even in everyday situations. But when he does, he becomes very agitated and upset – and blames others for what happens.

This offender is determined and mission oriented. Even under stress he is able to complete his assaults on his victims – which was his intention when he entered their residences. This ability to be cool under pressure is also a trait that those who know him have seen in the past. At times, when others are upset, and unable to function, he will appear unaffected and detached.

REAL LIFE CRIMINAL PROFILING QUESTIONS

Profiling is not just about asking questions. It's about asking the right set of questions of a particular case. It's important to remember that every crime is different, so every set of profile questions will be different, too.

Here are some examples of the types of questions that might be asked by a profiler when investigating a murder case.

- Who is the victim?

- What is their risk level of becoming a victim of this type of crime?

- Has the victim received any threats or reported any unusual activity?

- Who are the victim's friends and enemies?

- What does the victim do for employment?

- Did the victim resist attack?

- Where is the crime scene?

- What kind of crime scene is it?

- Who has access to the crime scene?

- Are there any signs of forced entry?

- If there are no signs of forced entry, how did the offender get entry or access to the crime scene?

- If the crime scene is remote, who would know about it?

- How much foot or vehicle traffic is there around the crime scene?

- How much time did the offender spend at the crime scene?

- Was a weapon used?

- If a weapon was used, what kinds of wounds does the victim have?

REAL LIFE CRIMINAL PROFILING QUESTIONS

- Who owned the weapon?
- Was the weapon available at the crime scene or was it brought by the offender?
- When during the offence was the weapon used?
- Did the offender try to clean up any evidence at the crime scene?
- Did the offender try to change the evidence to throw investigators off track?
- Is there any evidence to suggest there was more than one offender?
- If so, how many offenders are there?
- Did the offender bring anything else to the scene with them?
- Did they use any of the materials they brought with them?
- Did the offender say anything to the victim during the offence?

- What did the offender say?
- What was the tone of the offender's voice?
- What did the offender do when the victim struggled or resisted?
- Was the offender hurt during the offence?
- If so, how was the offender hurt and where?
- What is the available evidence in the crime?
- Has all of the evidence been made available to the profiler?
- If some material isn't available, why not?
- Is this material still available, and if not, why not?
- Who interpreted the crime scene evidence?
- What are their qualifications?

Glossary

autopsy: A medical examination of a corpse to determine the manner and cause of death. The word comes from the Greek *autós* (self) and *op* (see) – 'see for yourself'.

characteristic: A thing (such as a type of behaviour) that helps investigators separate a criminal from other people. Characteristics help investigators identify criminals.

detectives: Members of the police force who investigate cases and solve crimes.

ethics: The set of moral principles that govern the behaviour of a person, a group, or a profession.

evidence: Proof or disproof. It can be physical (blood, or weapons) or testimonial (witness statements).

forensic: Having to do with evidence in an investigation – a crime, an accident, a natural disaster, and so on.

modus operandi (MO): Functional things that a criminal has to do while carrying out a crime in order for the crime to be successful.

motive: The physical or psychological need that makes someone behave in a particular way.

murder (homicide): A manner of death in which one person kills another. Murder is the most serious way of causing the death of another person under the law. It can also be manslaughter (a less serious charge) or assisted suicide (helping someone die on purpose).

perpetrator: The person who commits a crime.

philosophers: People who study and practice the study of knowledge, reality, and existence.

prosecution: The lawyer or team of lawyers who try to prove that a defendant (the accused) is guilty. A guilty verdict is the same thing as a conviction.

psychiatrist: A medical practitioner who specialises in the diagnosis and treatment of mental illness, and matters relating to the mind.

psychologist: A person who practices psychology.

psychology: The scientific study of the human mind including its functions and how those functions affect human behaviour in a particular situation or during a particular activity.

statements: Verbal accounts of something that has happened. Following a crime, statements are taken from witnesses, victims, and suspects by a police officer or other investigator. A statement is then put into writing and becomes part of the evidence for that crime.

witnesses: The people who see something happen.

BOOKS

Mystery stories are a great way to learn how to think like a detective, especially the cases of Sherlock Holmes, written by Sir Arthur Conan Doyle. These books, below, are nonfiction guides.

The Forensic Casebook: The Science of Crime Scene Investigation, by N.E. Genge (Ballantine, 2002). This detailed text is peppered with the true tales of C.S.I.s, detectives and other experts. The sections on crime science careers and training are excellent.

Forensics, by Richard Platt. (Kingfisher/Houghton Mifflin, 2005). How to process a crime scene, measure ballistics (bullets and other projectiles), tell counterfeit money from real money and more.

Detective Science: 40 Crime-Solving, Case-Breaking, Crook-Catching Activities for Kids, by Jim Wiese (Jossey-Bass, 1996). How to collect trace evidence, lift fingerprints, make tooth impressions and other hands-on activities.

Crime Scene: How Investigators Use Science to Track Down the Bad Guys by Vivien Bowers, (Maple Tree Press, 2006) How toolmarks and fibres provide evidence, how to detect fake money and forgery and learn the ways in which clues, suspects and victims are connected.

WEBSITES

Access Excellence's The Mystery Spot:
Online or downloadable fictional mysteries for you to solve that rely on science.
http://www.accessexcellence.org/AE/mspot/

CourtTV's Forensic Files:
A database and case files of forensic investigating techniques – fingerprints, DNA, hair and fibre evidence and so on.
http://www.courttv.com/onair/shows/forensicfiles/ glossary/1.html

The FBI's Page for Kids:
Activities and games from the Federal Bureau of Investigation, the US government office that investigates federal crimes.
http://www.fbi.gov/kids/6th12th/6th12th.htm

Publisher's note to teachers and parents:
Our editors have carefully reviewed these websites to ensure that they are suitable for children. Many websites change frequently, however, and we cannot guarantee that a site's future contents will continue to meet our high standards of quality and educational value. Be advised that children should be closely supervised whenever they access the Internet.

Index